Vol II

Improving Your Vocabulary
One Word at a Time

Auntie Bev

AUNTIE BEV

WORDUP!

For permission, contact:
auntiebev@allwordzmatter.com

Cover designed by Ginger Marks,
DocUmeant Designs, LLC
www.docuMeantDesigns.com

Formatted by Editorjulz
editorjulz@gmail.com

ISBN: 978-0-977-8876-3-7

A Message from Auntie Bev.

Welcome to the WordUp! Vocabulary Dictionary Volume II. Hopefully, you've already started depositing into your vocabulary bank with Volume. 1.

This resource guide is slightly different from the first one, in that the words are more suitable for your professional conversations. Plus, in the beginning of this dictionary there is a refresher on the proper usage of **adjectives and adverbs,** along with a little quiz to test your knowledge beginning on page 11.

AUNTIE BEV

In addition, some of the words were submitted by my social media followers and I would like to acknowledge and say THANK YOU to them for their submissions:

Tae Capers

Jan Ellis

Byron Hairston

Jerelyn Hammer

Angela Wells Kidd

Nancy Kirkley

Sheri Luckett

Michael MacNeil

WORDUP!

Betsy Reinhart

I also want to thank Beverley Cornish, Raven Grisham, Sara Nunez Nogg, Vickie Maloney and Dorina Woffard for agreeing to review Volume II. I appreciate their comments and editing suggestions.

"The definitions and sample sentences provided in this dictionary would assist middle and high school students to understand the words more readily than the more formal dictionaries found in their classrooms."
~Beverley Cornish

Your usage examples excellently lend to the definitions. To be honest, this content could benefit a variety of age groups. My 60+ yo husband is in aircraft maintenance, feels he may have some subtle learning differences so is not a word geek. As an adult, he values learning new words and can definitely benefit from this. ~ Vickie Maloney

Here's some of the feedback I received from Volume 1:

"This dictionary is an excellent tool for anyone looking to improve their vocabulary. I love it. I try to use a word from it daily." ~Michelle

"Super awesome book for those wanting to increase their grammar and knowledge." ~Jamie

I actually had one young man tell me it was probably the only book he was ever going to read! I hope he was being **facetious** about that (lol!).

I sincerely appreciate all of your support.

WORDUP!

Remember, It's Your Time, Your Shine!

Auntie Bev. Speaks

Introduction

A strong vocabulary helps develop all four language skills: reading, writing, listening and speaking. In addition, your vocabulary plays a vital role in your ability to communicate your thoughts and ideas with clarity. The power of the words you speak and write also helps you to persuade others in your personal or professional life.

Here are the Top 5 reasons vocabulary is so important:

1) Improves Reading Comprehension. Research has shown that you need to understand 98% of the words you read to understand what you are reading.

WORDUP!

Improving vocabulary skills will improve your understanding of novels and textbooks.

2) Increases Language Development.
People who develop a strong vocabulary bank tend to be deeper thinkers, express themselves better, and read more. Improving language and literacy skills help you become more successful personally and professionally.

3) Effective Verbal Communication.
Successful communication or "saying what you mean" is dependent upon a good vocabulary bank. Using the right words when talking, makes you a more effective communicator.

4) Develop Expressive Writing Habits.
Having a strong vocabulary to draw from can help you write more effectively and creatively.

Students, especially, need to use a more formal tone when writing – not conversational language – and to do that, they need a richer vocabulary to tap into those words we don't use when we speak. Having a strong vocabulary also helps you to express your thoughts and ideas with clarity. Note: We should not write like we speak.

5) Occupational Success. Researcher Johnson O'Connor found that "a person's vocabulary level is the best single predictor of occupational success." Success in the business place depends on your communication skills.

Now, before you dig into the dictionary, let's go over some basics: **Adjectives vs. Adverbs**

WORDUP!

Adjectives are words that describe nouns (or pronouns). "Old", "red", and "cheerful" are examples of adjectives.

Adverbs are words that modify verbs, adjectives and other adverbs. They tell us how, when, where, to what extent and why. Adverbs often end in -ly.

Sentence Examples:

I **frequently** shop online because it's easier. (to what extent)

He ran **quickly**. (how)

She arrived **early** for the meeting. (when)

He drives **carefully** to avoid getting in an accident. (how)

AUNTIE BEV

It's extremely **hot**! (to what extent).

I **seldom** ride the bus. (to what extent)

WORDUP!

Adjectives Adverbs Quiz

1. Your blue skirt is _____the one you've got on, Mary; why don't you change?

A) much worse than

B) the best of

C) much nicer than

D) as better as

E) more expensive than

2. He's one of_____ people I've ever met. He never stops talking and never says anything.

_____.

A) the least bored/interested

B) the more boring/interesting

C) the most boring/interesting

D) the more bored/interested

E) the least boring/interested

3. He has got _____big feet _____he has difficulty finding shoes to fit him.

A) as/as

B) such/as

C) so/that

D) such/that

WORDUP!

E) more/than

4. You looked _____this morning,
but you look _____ now.

A) depressing/a lot happier

B) happier/a bit depressing

C) depressed/much happy

D) depressed/a bit happier

E) a bit happier/more depressing

5. _____electricity you use,
_____ your bill will be.

A) The more/the lower

B) The less/the higher

C) The more/the higher

D) The most/the lowest

E) The least/the highest **Verbs and Verb Tenses:**

How did you do? (answers in the back of the book).

OK...now to keep building your vocabulary bank with Volume II of: Auntie Bev's WordUp! Personalized Vocabulary Dictionary.

WordUp! Vocabulary List

A

Absolve

Alleviate

Ambiguous

Arduous

Ascertain

Atrocious (submitted by Tae Capers)

Averse

B

Belittle

Berate

Bias

Bolster

Brash

C

Callous

Chastise

Coalesce

Cognizant

WORDUP!

Commiserate

Contrite (submitted by Angela Wells Kidd)

Cunning

D

Debonair

Digress

Disdain

Disingenuous (submitted by Nancy Kirtley)

Dissent

E

Effervescent (submitted by Byron Hairston)

Egregious

Empathy

Engrossed

Erudite

Exemplify

F

Fallacious

Feasible

Fervent

WORDUP!

Frugal

Fugacious

G

Garrulous

Gullible

Grudge

H

Haggle

Harridan

Harrowing

Heinous

Hinder

Hypocorism

I

Idoneous

Immense

Impinge (Besty Reinhart)

Injudicious

Inveterate

Invidious

J

Jargon

Jeer

Jeopardize

Justify

K

Keen

Kudos

L

Lachrymose

Lackadaisical

Libel

Livid

M

Malice

Meretricious

Metaphor

Mollify

Morose

Mundane

N

Nadir

Naught

Nefarious (submitted by Sheri Luckett)

Nonchalant

O

Oblivious

Obsolete

Obstreperous

Ostentatious

Ostracize

P

Parsimonious

Patronize

Petulant

Paucity

Platitude (submitted by Michael MacNeil)

Precarious

Preposterous

Prevaricate

Q

Quaint

Quell

Quiescent

R

Rambunctious

Recluse

Reciprocate

Refute

Reiterate

Relentless

AUNTIE BEV

Ruminate

Repugnant

S

Salubrious

Satire

Scrutinize

Sedulous

Simile

Squander

Stagnant

Surreal (Jan Ellis)

T

Tact

Taunt

Tenable

Tenacity

Traduce

Transcend

Trepidation

U

Ultimatum

Uncouth

Unkempt

Unravel

V

Vacate

Vim

Validate

Vicarious

W

Waive

Wallow

WORDUP!

Wary

Wreak

Y

Yearn/Yearning

Z

Zeal

Zest

Bonus Words

Aplomb

Diligent

Dynamic

Indelible

Methodical

Motivated

Rescind

WORDUP!

A

Absolve (ab-solv) (verb) To declare or set someone free from guilt or responsibility.

Sentence example: The suspect maintained his innocence throughout his trial and hoped the jury would **absolve** him of the burglary charges because he was facing 25 years in prison.

Alleviate (uh-lee-ve-ate) (verb) To make something less painful, less severe.

Sentence example: Food banks are established in many communities to help **alleviate** hunger.

Bonus sentence: Megan thought it was best to apologize to her mother to **alleviate** further hostility between them.

Ambiguous (am-big-u-us) (adj) Unclear or confusing because it could have more than one meaning.

Sentence example: Sometimes weather forecasters make **ambiguous** statements when they say partly cloudy. Does that mean it will be partly sunny too?

Bonus sentence: I thought Mark gave me **ambiguous** directions when told me to drive down the main street and then turn right on Main Street.

WORDUP!

Arduous (r-joo-us) (adj) Requiring a strenuous effort.

Sentence: Mountain climbing is an **arduous** task.

Ascertain (ass-er-tane) (verb) To find out something for certain; to make sure of or determine.

Sentence example: A study was conducted to ascertain if there was a connection between gender and low wages.

Bonus sentence: In order to **ascertain** the truth about whether his wife was cheating, Jeremy hired a private investigator to follow her around.

Atrocious (ah-tro-shus) Heinous; wicked.

Sentence example: When Roseanne sang the National Anthem at a baseball game in 1990, many people thought her singing was atrocious.

Bonus sentence: Putting razor blades in apples and giving them out to Trick or Treaters during Halloween is an **atrocious** act!

Averse (uh-verse) (verb) Having a strong dislike or opposition to something.

Sentence example: Some people are vegetarians; that's why they are **averse** to eating meat.

WORDUP!

B

Belittle (be-little) (verb) To make someone feel unimportant or worthless.

Sentence example: Sarah refused to allow her parents to continue to belittle her, so she ran away from home and joined the circus.

Bonus sentence: When someone tries to **belittle** you, they often feel bad about their own life.

Berate (be-rate) (verb) To scold or criticize someone in an angry and loud way.

Sentence example: The teacher decided to **berate** the student in front of the class because he didn't turn in his homework assignment.

Bonus sentence: The manager chose to berate any employee who didn't show up for work at least 10 minutes early.

Bias (by-us) (noun) Prejudice in favor of or against something or someone in comparison with another.

Sentence example: The football coach showed his **bias** when he decided to start his son as the quarterback although he had never played the position before.

Bonus sentence: It is sad when you let your **bias** stand in the way of getting to know people from other cultures.

WORDUP!

Bolster (bowl-stir) (verb) To support or strengthen.

Sentence example: The high school football team wanted to **bolster** tickets to their games by offering free snacks.

Bonus sentence: Maria tried to **bolster** her opportunity for a promotion by working longer hours and taking on more responsibility.

Brash (brash) (adj) Assertive in an aggressive or rude way.

Sentence example: Employers who have a **brash** personality are difficulty to work for.

AUNTIE BEV

Bonus sentence: I didn't appreciate the pushiness of the **brash** salesman when he was trying to sell me a car.

WORDUP!

C

Callous (cal-us) (adj) Insensitive and cruel disregard for others.

Sentence example: The **callous** doctor had no problem telling the patient he was fat and lazy.

Chastise (chas-tize) To criticize someone harshly for doing something wrong.

Sentence example: If the manager catches you texting or watching videos at work, she will **chastise** you and you might end up getting fired.

Bonus sentence: Some parents spend a lot of time having to **chastise** their children for getting in trouble at school.

Coalesce (Co-a-less) (verb) To come together as a single mass or as a whole.

Sentence example: All of the neighbors decided to **coalesce** to welcome the new family into the neighborhood.

Bonus sentence: When Martin and Jill announced they were getting married, the two families put their differences aside and opted to **coalesce** for the good of the couple.

Cognizant (cog-na-zent) (adj) To be aware of; to have knowledge.

Sentence example: It is important to be **cognizant** of your surroundings if you are in an unfamiliar area.

WORDUP!

Commiserate (cuh-miz-er-ate) (verb) To express or feel sympathy or pity.

Sentence example: After losing the championship, the football team decided to **commiserate** their feelings by running 10 laps up and down the football field.

Bonus sentence: After Anna's son left for college, Anna was determined not to **commiserate** over the fact that she was becoming an empty nester.

Contrite: (con-trite) (adj) Feeling or expressing remorse; a guilty conscience.

Sentence example: After being sentenced to 20 years in prison for armed robbery, the defendant looked at the victim and was visibly **contrite.**

Cunning (cuh-ning) Sly or crafty; deceitful.

Sentence example: Tony developed a reputation for being a shrewd businessman because he was so **cunning** in his dealing with customers.

WORDUP!

D

Debonair (deb-ah-nair) (adj) Confident, stylish.

Sentence example: Jordan Poole looks quite **debonair** when he's wearing those Warby Parker glasses.

Bonus sentence: Monica was quite surprised to see how **debonair** Rico looked at church because he normally dresses like he has no fashion sense.

Digress (die-gress) (verb) Going off topic temporarily to distract from talking about a subject.

Sentence example: Lucy would **digress** every time her parents asked about how she was doing in college.

Bonus: Some politicians choose to **digress** when you ask them for specifics on how they are representing their constituents.

Disdain (dis-dane) A lack of respect or contempt for someone or something you believe is inferior.

Sentence example as a noun: The **disdain** shown to immigrants by some people is disgraceful.

Sentence example as a verb: Jennifer told her mother-in-law she had a **disdain** for her drinking alcohol while babysitting her grandchildren.

WORDUP!

Disingenuous (dis-in-gin-u-us) (adj) Not candid or sincere by pretending to know less about a situation than you actually do.

Sentence example: Monica knew her sister's boyfriend was cheating on her but she was disingenuous about sharing what she knew because she knew her sister would be crushed.

Bonus sentence: A **disingenuous** person will make you believe they're a good friend in order to take advantage of your kindheartedness.

Dissent (dis-sent) (verb) To differ in opinion.

Sentence example: When a majority rules on the Supreme Court, the justices, who were in the minority, normally offer a **dissenting** opinion on why they didn't vote with the majority.

Bonus sentence:

It's OK to **dissent** on an issue, but you should never let it turn into a heated argument or a fight.

E

Effervescent (effer-ves-cent) (adj) This word has two definitions: Vivacious and enthusiastic; something fizzy and bubbly.

Sentence example: The **effervescent** cheap wine tickeled my nose.

Sentence example: Patricia was selected homecoming queen because she has such an **effervescent** personality.

Egregious (eh-gree-jus) Horrifying, shocking.

Sentence example: The judge told the defendant his crime was the most **egregious** act he'd ever heard in his courtroom.

Empathy (M-puh-thee) (noun) The ability to understand and share the feelings of someone else.

Sentence example: The teacher showed no **empathy** when the student told her that her dog ate her homework.

Engrossed (in-grossed) (adj)To be preoccupied with; giving your undivided attention to something.

Sentence example: I was completely **engrossed** in that book because it was so good!

WORDUP!

Erudite (air-ya-dite) (adj) Having or showing great knowledge.

Sentence example: Louise is an **erudite** librarian who can help you find the right books on any subject.

Exemplify (x-m-plah-fy) (verb) To show or illustrate by example.

Sentence example: The manager told the new employees they were expected to **exemplify** good work habits by showing up for work at least 10 minutes early and working overtime when necessary.

F

Fallacious (fa-lay-shus) (adj) Capable of making mistakes or being wrong.

Sentence example: Dr. Jackson apologized to the patient for being **fallacious** when he incorrectly diagnosed her with breast cancer.

Feasible (feez-ah-bowl) (adj) Able to do without much difficulty.

Sentence example: It is not **feasible** to drive a vehicle down the highway with your eyes closed.

Bonus sentence: It is **feasible** for us to take a family cruise to the Bahamas if we all chip in five hundred dollars.

Fervent (fur-vent) (adj) A passionate intensity.

Sentence example: Martin's **fervent** love of math is the reason he wanted to become an accountant.

Frugal (fru-gul) (adj) careful in spending money.

Sentence example: Dorothy is a **frugal** shopper who loves clipping and using coupons when she buys groceries.

Fugacious (few-gay-shus) (adj) Short-lived; a fleeting moment.

Sentence example: Penny told her boyfriend she didn't want flowers for Valentine's Day because they were too **fugacious**. She preferred a diamond bracelet instead.

G

Garrulous (gare-ah-lus) (adj) Excessively talkative on trivial matters.

Sentence example: It's never a good thing to sit next to a **garrulous** person on a long flight because you will never get any rest.

Gullible (gul-ah-bowl) (adj) Easily persuaded to believe something whether it's true or not; easily fooled.

Sentence example: Catfish is a popular TV show because there are so many **gullible** men and women who are looking for love in all the wrong places.

AUNTIE BEV

Grudge (grudge/sounds like fudge) (adj) A deep dislike or animosity towards someone who you believe treated you unfairly in the past.

Sentence example: At her 40th high school reunion, Cassie was still holding onto an old **grudge** against Tonya and refused to speak to her. Cassie was upset because Tonya stole her boyfriend in the 11th grade.

H

Haggle (hag-ul) (verb) To engage in a conversation persistently in an attempt to reach a deal.

Sentence example: Why do some people **haggle** over prices at a flea market when the prices are already cheap?

Harridan (hare-ih-dun) (noun) A bossy older woman who is difficult to deal with.

Sentence example: Grandma was a **harridan** who made everyone feel uncomfortable when they were around her.

AUNTIE BEV

Harrowing (hair-o-wing) (adj) Very distressing.

Sentence example: Going into a haunted house during Halloween can be a very **harrowing** experience!

Heinous (hane-us) (adj) Wicked; shockingly evil, hateful act.

Sentence example: Some wives might consider their husbands forgetting their wedding anniversary as a **heinous** act.

Hinder (hen-dur) (verb) Create difficulties to stop someone from accomplishing something.

Sentence example: Don't let anyone **hinder** you from achieving your goals and dreams.

WORDUP!

Hypocorism (hi-poc-or-izm) (noun) A pet name of a nickname.

Sentence example: For years, people thought Reggie's first name was Bubba, but it was a **hypocorism** given by his grandfather because he was very chubby as a baby.

I

Idoneous (eye-doe-ne-us) (adj) Appropriate, suitable, qualified.

Sentence example: Brandy was the most **idoneous** teacher for our French class because she spent five years living there.

Immense (e-mence) (adj) Extremely large or great in size or degree.

Sentence example: The African American History Museum in Washington, DC is an **immense** building with lots of artifacts dating back to the Transatlantic Slave Trade.

WORDUP!

Impinge (m-pinje) (verb) To have an effect or impact, which is usually negative.

Sentence example: Larry's excessive drinking at night is starting to **impinge** on his ability to get up and get to work on time.

Injudicious (in-ju-dish-us) (adj) Showing poor judgement.

Sentence example: I made some **injudicious** decisions as a teenager but, thankfully, I grew up and became wiser.

Invective (in-vek-tiv) (noun) Insulting, abusive language used to criticize.

Sentence example: The **invective** coming from the politician's mouth during the rally made a number of people get up and leave.

Inveterate (in-vetter-ut) (adj) Having a particular interest or habit that is unlikely to change.

Sentence example: Ever since Rachel was a little girl, she wanted to be a nurse because she always had an **inveterate** desire to take care of others.

Invidious (in-vid-ee-us) (adj) Likely to cause bad feelings in other people.

Sentence example: When Victor drinks alcohol, he exhibits **invidious** behavior by insulting everyone around him.

J

Jargon (jar-gun) (adj) Specialized language used by a particular group of people.

Sentence example: The lawyer tried to impress the audience with all of her legal **jargon**, but she ended up putting a lot of people to sleep because her speech was so boring.

Jeopardize (jep-or-dize) (verb) To put something or someone in a situation where there is danger of a loss or harm.

Sentence example: Ben didn't want to **jeopardize** getting a promotion at work, so he worked extra-long hours to try to impress the boss.

AUNTIE BEV

Juncture (junk-sure) (noun) An important point in a process or activity.

Sentence example: At this **juncture** we need to look for additional funding for our home renovations because the project has exceeded our budget.

Justify (jus-tih-fy) (verb) To offer a reasonable explanation for a certain behavior or action.

Sentence example: The HR Dept at Tammy's job told her she needed to **justify** her injuries by producing some medical bills before she could file for worker's compensation.

WORDUP!

K

Keen (keen) (adj) Demonstrating a strong or highly developed sense.

Sentence example: Dogs tend to have a **keen** sense of smell.

Bonus sentence: Monica had a **keen** observation of her surroundings and that's why she was able to identify a man who was about to rob the bank where she worked.

Kudos (koo-dos) (noun) Praise and recognition received for an achievement.

Sentence: Patricia received **kudos** for receiving the only perfect score on the science test.

L

Lachrymose (lack-rih-mos) (adj) Easily brought to tears.

Sentence example: Every time I watch the movie, Stepmom, I am always **lachrymose** when Julia Roberts' character dies near the end.

Lackadaisical (lack-ah-daze-ih-kul) (adj) Lacking enthusiasm or interest, lazy.

Sentence example: After losing his job, Pablo became very **lackadaisical** and slept until 4:00 in the afternoon every day.

WORDUP!

Lacuna (la-coon-ah) (noun) A missing part, a gap.

Sentence example: Richard explained the reason he has a three-year **lacuna** in his resume was because he went on an overseas mission trip to Uganda.

Libel (lie-bul) (noun) A published false statement about someone that views them in a negative light.

Sentence example: Jennifer filed a **libel** lawsuit against her local TV station after they falsely identified her as the teacher who made a student, suffering from cerebral (suh-ree-brul) palsy get out of his wheelchair and walk to the bathroom. Her name was Jennifer Johnson. The person who actually did it was named Jennifer Jonson (minus the "h").

Livid (liv-id) (adj) Furiously angry.

Sentence example: After his team lost, Adam was **livid** and threw a baseball bat at the TV screen.

M

Malicious (ma-lish-us) (adj) Intentionally harmful.

Darcy didn't understand why her friends were making **malicious** comments on a video she posted on TikTok showing her taking a bath.

Manipulate (ma-nip-u-late) (adj) To try to control or handle something or someone.

Sentence example: The used car salesman tried to **manipulate** the elderly couple into spending more money on a vehicle that had been in three previous accidents.

Meretricious (mare-ah-trish-us) (adj)
Attractive on the outside but having no real
substance or value.

Sentence example: Janice thought her
popularity and beauty would make her the
next homecoming queen, but her classmates
called her a **meretricious** snob who only had
friends because she had money.

Mundane (mun-dane) (adj) Dull, boring, not
interesting.

Sentence example: My history teacher is so
mundane, which probably explains why I'm
failing in the class.

N

Nadir (nay-dur) (noun) all-time low, hit rock bottom.

Sentence example: Employee morale hit a **nadir** when they learned they would not be receiving Christmas bonuses this year.

Nefarious (na-fare-ee-us) (adj) Evil, wicked or criminal.

Sentence example: Sandra was a **nefarious** bully towards everyone in high school until she met Lilly, who beat her up and locked her in the janitor's closet.

Nonchalant (non-sha-launt) Cool, calm, relaxed, unphased.

Sentence example: When Amy saw Derrick, she tried to act **nonchalant**, but she was anxious for him to ask her to go out on a date.

O

Oblivious (o-bliv-ee-us) (adj) Not aware of or concerned with what is happening around you.

Sentence example: Terri was **oblivious** to the fact she wore a pink outfit to a "White Party."

Obsolete (ob-suh-leet) (adj) No longer used; out of date.

Sentence example: Many people used to have a home telephone, but they have become **obsolete** and been replaced by cellphones.

Obstreperous (ob-strep-per-us) (adj) Noisy and difficult to control.

Sentence example: When Frank drinks too many beers, he becomes **obstreperous.**

Bonus sentence: When Jack saw someone trying to steal his car in front of his house, he was **obstreperous** and threatened to beat up the thief with a baseball bat.

Ostentatious (os-ten-tay-shus) (adj) Intended to attract attention in an extreme or obvious way.

Sentence example: Everyone at church thought Tiffany was being quite **ostentatious** when she showed up every week, during the summer, wearing a very expensive looking fur coat.

P

Parsimonious (par-sih-mo-nee-us) (adj)
Don't like to spend money; stingy.

Sentence example: Phil was a **parsimonious** man who couldn't keep a girlfriend because he didn't like to spend money on dates.

Paucity (paw-sih-tee) (noun) A small amount of something; insufficient quantity.

Sentence example: You're not going to be able to drive to the grocery store with only a **paucity** of gas.

Platitude (platuh-tude) (noun) Something that has been repeated so often that it loses its meaning or impact.

Platitude examples: "All that glitters is not gold." "It is what it is." "Time heals all wounds."

Precarious (pre-care-ee-us) (adj) Unstable, dangerous or difficult.

Sentence example: Linda found herself in a **precarious** situation when she ran out of gas on the highway at midnight.

Prevaricate (pra-vare-uh-kate) (verb) To speak or act in an evasive way.

Sentence example: When you **prevaricate**, you can make a disagreement worse than it already is.

Q

Quaint (kwaint) (adj) Charming, old fashioned.

Sentence example: My family rented a **quaint** Air BNB in the Blue Ridge Mountains.

Qualitative (kwal-ih-tae-tiv) (adj) Measuring something by quality rather than quantity.

Sentence example: There are **qualitative** differences in the way men and women view a girls' night out versus a guys' night out.

Quiescent (kwee-es-sent) (adj) Not active;
quiet

Sentence example: Ms. Taylor was enjoying
the **quiescent** time because soon her day
would be consumed by 25 active
preschoolers.

R

Rambunctious (ram-bunk-shus) (adj) Hyper and overly energetic.

Sentence example: Darla was a **rambunctious** three-year-old who was always getting into trouble at her daycare.

Reciprocate (re-sip-pro-kate) (verb) To give back in return.

Sentence example: If someone does something nice for you, you should try to **reciprocate** their kindness or pay it forward to someone else.

Reiterate (re-it-er-rate) (verb)To repeat something more than once to emphasize or give clarity.

Sentence example: William's dad felt it was necessary to **reiterate** the dangers of drunk driving.

Relentless (re-lent-less) (adj) Persistent; constant.

Sentence example: Adam was **relentless** in his efforts to make the football team, so he practiced drills for six hours every day.

Repugnant (re-pug-nunt) (adj) Extremely distasteful; offensive.

Sentence example: The smell in the gas station bathroom was so **repugnant**, it made me throw up!

WORDUP!

Bonus sentence: Ethan's **repugnant** behavior in school got him kicked out for the year and he ended up having to repeat the 10th grade.

S

Salubrious (suh-lu-bree-us) (adj) Something that is good for you; beneficial to the mind and body.

Sentence example: Every year, Eve makes the same New Year's resolution: to go on a **salubrious** diet but she always stops after a few weeks.

Scrutinize (screw-tin-eyes) (verb) To examine or inspect closely and thoroughly.

Sentence example: Before you purchase a used car, it's best to **scrutinize** it to make sure you're not buying a lemon.

WORDUP!

Sedulous (said-joo-lus) (adj) Demonstrating dedication and diligence; hardworking.

Sentence example: The manager loved Alice because she was a **sedulous** employee, but she decided to retire after 30 years on the job.

Simile (sim-ah-lee) (noun) A figure of speech that compares two things, using the words "like" "as" or "than."

Simile examples: "Busy as a bee" "Cold as ice" "Fat as a pig" "Stubborn as a mule" "Sweet as honey."

Squander (sqwan-der) (verb) To waste something in a reckless and foolish manner.

Sentence example: Do not **squander** time because life is short.

AUNTIE BEV

Surreal (sir-real) (adj) Appearing as a fantasy or dream; a little on the bizarre side.

Sentence example: Patty said, during her surgery, she had a **surreal** experience by seeing a place she thought was Heaven. She also said she saw her grandparents sitting in a garden and they invited her to join them.

WORDUP!

T

Tact (tact) (noun) The ability to say or do things in such a way that doesn't upset or offend anyone.

Sentence example: Some politicians lack **tact** and don't know how to relate to their constituents.

Bonus sentence: Even though Barbara was always mean to Laura at work, she used **tact** when she learned Laura's mother had died.

Taunt (taunt) (verb) To intentionally annoy or upset someone by saying nasty things to trigger a response.

Sentence example: Some people try to **taunt** others on social media because they can hide behind the computer.

Tenable (ten-ah-bowl) Able to be maintained, defended, or protected without objection.

Sentence example: The suspect tried to bribe a friend to give him a **tenable** alibi to keep him from going to prison for armed robbery.

Tenacity (ten-ass-sit-ee) (noun) Determined to do or achieve something; to have a firm grip.

Sentence example: You need **tenacity** in order to pursue your goals, especially when you are facing obstacles.

WORDUP!

Terse (rhymes with purse) (adj) Short response or remark that comes across as angry.

Sentence example: When submitting her resignation, Samantha had some **terse** words for her employer about what she thought of the way he treated her.

Transcend (tran-send) (verb) To go beyond the limits or surpass.

Sentence example: Phil wanted to get a PhD in Physics because he wanted to **transcend** his knowledge of science.

AUNTIE BEV

Trepidation (trep-ih-day-shun) (noun) A feeling of fear or nervousness about something that may happen.

Sentence example: Joan was filled with **trepidation** as she prepared to go ziplining for the first time.

Tumultuous (too-mull-choo-us) Making a loud noise; an uproar.

Sentence example: On New Year's Eve, there is always a **tumultuous** celebration in Times Square in New York City.

U

Ultimatum (ul-tim-ate-um) (noun) A final demand or statement of terms offered with retaliation if demand is rejected.

Sentence example: Gloria gave her daughter an **ultimatum:** if she didn't clean the kitchen all week, she wouldn't be allowed to go to the school dance.

Uncouth (un-cooth) (adj) Lacking in good manners; behavior not acceptable.

Sentence example: It is **uncouth** to ask someone how much they paid for your Christmas gift.

Bonus example: Marcus wanted to marry Wendy, but his parents thought she was an

uncouth young woman because she refused to use silverware when eating.

Unkempt (un-kempt) (adj) Unclean or untidy.

Sentence example: Kim's children always look so **unkempt** in public, but Kim is always dressed to the nines.

Bonus sentence: Everyone thought Mr. Harper was homeless because he was always **unkempt,** but he dressed that way because he didn't want anyone to know how wealthy he really was.

WORDUP!

Unravel (un-rav-ul) (verb) To undo; to come apart.

Sentence example: Vanessa's story about being kidnapped began to **unravel** when she kept changing her story about the description of the suspect and how he managed to get her in his car as he was driving down the street.

V

Vacate (vay-kate) (verb) To leave; to move out of.

Sentence example: The landlord told the tenant to **vacate** the apartment immediately because she had not paid rent for the past three months.

Vim (vim) (noun) Energy, enthusiasm.

Sentence example: After losing 30 pounds, Jessica was full of **vim** and vigor.

Validate (val-ih-date) (verb) To check or prove the accuracy or truth of something.

Sentence example: In order to **validate** the news story, the reporter checked several sources to make sure they all identified the same suspect.

Vicarious (vi-care-ee-us) (adj) Experiencing your life by watching, listening or reading about another person.

Sentence example: Max said he experienced **vicarious** pain when his wife was pregnant with their twins.

W

Wallow (wall-oh) (verb) To get caught up in your emotions; generally, a sad or angry emotion.

Sentence example: Anna couldn't help but **wallow** in self-pity after learning she didn't win the homecoming queen contest.

Witless (wit-less) (adj) Foolish; stupid.

Sentence example: Norman was known at work as a **witless** employee who always photocopied his lunch and sent it to his mother so she would make sure he was eating healthy.

Wreak (reek) (verb) To cause a large amount of damage or harm.

Sentence example: If the internet goes down, it will **wreak** havoc for people who rely on it for their business.

Y

Yearn (verb) Have an intense feeling or longing for something or someone.

Yearning (noun)

Sentence example (verb): I **yearn** for the day when I don't have to work anymore and can just travel anywhere I want.

Sentence example (noun): Eva told James she was **yearning** for his love and wanted to know why he didn't seem interested in her.

Z

Zeal (zeel) (noun) Great energy or enthusiasm for a cause or objective.

Sentence example: Barry's **zeal** and passion for civil rights is the reason he won the award for Advocate of the Year.

Bonus Words

Aplomb

Diligent

Disparage

Dynamic

Malice

Recondite

Rescind

WORDUP!

Aplomb (uh-plum) (noun) Showing self-confidence and skill in challenging situations.

Sentence example: With **aplomb**, Tyrone was able to fight off a shark attack in the ocean without an injury.

Corpulent (core-pew-lent) (adj) Fat.

Sentence example: I always thought Santa Claus was **corpulent** until I realized he had a pillow stuffed inside his outfit.

Diligent (dill-a-jent) (adj) Someone who is diligent works hard and carefully.

Sentence example: Marty told the interviewer he was a **diligent** person who always took his job very seriously.

AUNTIE BEV

Disparage (dis-pair-ij) (verb) To express a negative opinion; to belittle.

Sentence example: It's never a good idea to **disparage** someone you hardly know.

Dynamic (die-nam-ik) (adj) a person who has a positive attitude, full of energy, and generates new ideas.

Sentence example: Phyllis has such a **dynamic** personality, which makes it easy for people to talk with her.

Mellifluous (ma-lif-lu-us) (adj) A smooth, flowing sound pleasing to the ear.

Sentence example: I love going to church to hear the **mellifluous** choir.

WORDUP!

Recondite (wreck-cun-dite) (adj) Not very well known or understood.

Sentence example: The Alice in Wonderland syndrome is a **recondite** neurological disorder that you probably have never heard of.

Rescind (re-send) (verb) To revoke, cancel or repeal.

Sentence example: Victor decided to **rescind** his marriage proposal to April after he discovered she had lied to him about her age. She was 48 instead of 28, like she told him.

Answers to the Adjectives/Adverbs Quiz
from page 11 to 14.

1) C
2) C
3) D
4) D
5) C

There you have it. Get ready for Volume III!

Auntie Bev Speaks

WORDUP!

Sources Used:

Merriam-Webster online dictionary

Vocabulary.com

Words in a Sentence (wordsinasentence.com)

About the Author

BEVERLY MAHONE, also known as "Auntie Bev" to nearly 3 million followers across all social media platforms, is a veteran journalist who has spent more than 40 years in radio and television news. She has worked as a radio news anchor, talk show host, television reporter, videographer, and as an Assignment Editor. After leaving the business in 2006, She decided to create a media marketing consulting business where she coached baby boomer women on how to market and pro mote themselves for media exposure and how to create videos.

With her love for writing, Beverly has written several books, including 6 Amazon bestselling books, **Whatever! A Baby Boomer's Journey Into Middle Age** (2006), **How to Get on the News without Committing Murder** (2016), **The Baby Boomer/Millennial Divide: Making it Work** (2018), **How to Cuss with Class First and Second Edition** (2023) and **WordUp Vocabulary Dictionary Volume 1** (2024).

In her semi-retirement, she works as a part-time Writing Consultant at North Carolina Central University. She has appeared as a guest of the Kelly Clarkson Show and written for or been covered by HuffPost50, Forbes.com, and U.S. News and World Report. Her video podcast, The Boomer Beat, airs on YouTube. Beverly has been featured as a baby boomer expert on MSNBC-TV and in the New York Times newspaper. She has represented Google as an Influencer and collaborated with American Advisors Group, The History Channel, Kroger, Butterball Turkey and Butterball Turkey in various campaigns.

You can learn more about her by visiting her website: allwordzmatter.com.

Made in United States
Troutdale, OR
08/20/2025